Charles C. Abbott

Recent Archaeological Explorations in the Valley of the Delaware

Salzwasser

Charles C. Abbott

Recent Archaeological Explorations in the Valley of the Delaware

1. Auflage | ISBN: 978-3-84604-712-5

Erscheinungsort: Frankfurt, Deutschland

Erscheinungsjahr: 2020

Salzwasser Verlag GmbH

Reprint of the original, first published in 1892.

Frontispiece. VIEW OF BURLINGTON ISLAND: LOOKING NORTHEAST.

PUBLICATIONS OF THE UNIVERSITY OF PENNSYLVANIA

SERIES IN

Philology Literature and Archæology

Vol. II   No. 1

RECENT ARCHÆOLOGICAL EXPLORATIONS

IN THE

VALLEY OF THE DELAWARE

BY

CHARLES C. ABBOTT, M.D.

CURATOR, MUSEUM OF AMERICAN ARCHÆOLOGY
UNIVERSITY OF PENNSYLVANIA

1892

GINN & COMPANY

Agents for United States, Canada and England
7-13 Tremont Place, Boston, U.S.A.

MAX NIEMEYER

Agent for the Continent of Europe
Halle, a. S., Germany

THE Papers of this Series, prepared by Professors and others connected with the University of Pennsylvania, will take the form of Monographs on the subjects of Philology, Literature, and Archæology, whereof about 200 or 250 pages will form a volume.

The price to subscribers to the Series will be $1.50 per volume; to others than subscribers, $2.00 per volume.

Each Monograph, however, is complete in itself and will be sold separately.

It is the intention of the University to issue these Monographs from time to time as they shall be prepared.

Each author assumes the responsibility of his own contribution.

RECENT ARCHÆOLOGICAL EXPLORATIONS IN THE VALLEY OF THE DELAWARE

LATE in the summer of 1891 my field work consisted exclusively of a study of the valley of the Delaware River, its islands, gravel deposits, and recent alluvium, with reference to the subject of antiquity, or better, point of beginning, of the occupancy of this region by Man.

My principal points of exploration were the two large islands in the river, near the head of tide water; one, a short distance below Bordentown, New Jersey, and the other, that which lies between Burlington, New Jersey, and Bristol, Bucks County, Pennsylvania. These islands are identical in their physical characters, and any reference to relative position of underlying gravel and superficial soil, the presence of erratic boulders and effects of recent water action, is equally applicable to both.

How rapidly the bed and banks of the Delaware River are changing, although the forces now operating are as nothing compared to the floods of glacial and immediately post-glacial times, may be realized upon the examination of scattered ridges of fine gravel, commingled with which will be found abundant fragments of materials that through white men's agency have been brought within the range of the river's ordinary current or of occasional freshets. Thus, on the upper ends of the islands in the river will be found, in many places, quite extensive accumulations of small globular or oval pebbles, needing almost no force to carry them from point to point, moved from old gravel deposits and mingled with pebbles of very recent origin, as bits of glass, slag from furnaces, anthracite, and products of human industry established within the past two centuries. These most recent of all river deposits often overlie a considerable accumulation of soil, under which is sand, which rests upon that coarse gravel and boulders borne to its present resting-place by agencies that long ago ceased to be in operation. It is of much interest to note that in such recent gravel and rubbish beds objects of Indian origin do not occur. The transporting power of the river, since the entire disappearance of what may be termed glacial floods, has not been equal to lifting a large argillite implement, weighing two or three pounds, from the bed of the stream and carrying it a considerable distance, finally placing it at a higher level than that from which it came. If moved at all, it would be rolled over the pebbly bottom and finally lodged in protected mud-deposits. The result of this rolling is to wear away the evidences of artificial fracturing and re-convert the tool of primitive man into a pebble. That this has happened in innumerable instances is doubtless true, doubtful specimens occurring abundantly in the present bed of the river. Again, a thin angular object, like an arrow-head, is not likely to be moved by the force of even moderately rapidly running water. The scanty number of these objects in the bed of the river, and, more noticeably so, in the inflowing creeks, very soon became imbedded in firm mud, clay, or compacted gravel; this, naturally, by reason of their shape.

Examining, then, a deposit of gravel laid down within fifty years or less, we find abundant traces of the present people dwelling on the river shore; by delving more deeply, we find traces that unmistakably point to the Indian; and the question that has been often asked and more frequently answered negatively than affirmatively is, can we go still deeper and find equally convincing evidences of the Indian's predecessor, or more correctly, ancestor? [1]

The position that I have taken for many years is, that we can

---

[1] In remarking that this question has been answered negatively, I do not refer to disgraceful articles in pretentious periodicals, written by persons wholly ignorant of the subject. It is a blot upon American letters that editors should solicit from incompetency, however prominent politically, articles that their authors know are misleading. Unfortunately, the public cannot always discriminate.

do so, and of the reasonableness of this stand, I am more than ever persuaded, by reason of an unbiassed examination of the two islands that have been mentioned. For instance, we find on Burlington Island, a foundation of coarse gravel intermingled with large boulders, many weighing from two to four tons; material such as no freshet in historic times moves any appreciable distance, and within the range of tide water does not and cannot move at all; and at low tide there is exposed a wide gravel beach, which is but a continuation of the base of the island, that constitutes the bed of the stream, and extending westward, is the foundation of the cultivable soil on the Pennsylvania shore. It is evident at a glance that the island is but a heaping up of this gravel as a long, narrow ridge, and as years rolled by, the soil began to form, augmented by occasional muddy freshets that left a deposit of vegetation-supporting material, as now happens yearly over the low-lying meadows near by. Now, characteristic of this gravel, whenever examined, is the occurrence of rudely fashioned stone implements, — for no one capable of forming an opinion doubts their artificial origin, — and again, characteristic of the superficial soil, is the occurrence of pottery and arrow-points of stone, ornamental objects, and the hundred and one evidences of the Indian's varied handiwork. What, then, is the relationship of the two? Is or is not their separation a mere coincidence? Are they or are they not of one age and origin? We are bound, in all reasonableness, to adopt the most plausible explanation, and never are warranted in reaching from the known to the unknown. To do so, is to stand apart and quite out of touch with logical students. We have, as is well known, historic evidence in abundance, of the former presence of the Indian in the Delaware valley; and what ground is there, therefore, for referring to some unknown people what is undoubtedly within Indian capabilities, and, indeed, characteristic of that people? There is none whatever; but does the claim that certain rude stone implements point to what is known as "palæolithic man" demand another than the Indian as a resident of this river valley? I think not. The question simply is, — has man risen from a palæolithic to a neolithic condition while living in this valley? or do the conditions point to the use of rude and elaborate implements alike, at the same time?

As a matter of necessity, all unquestionable Indian implements are not of the same age. This Indian occupied the river valley in that stage of culture in which he was discovered by Europeans, for many centuries; and the process of implement-making was continuous throughout that time, and evidence of an advance in the tool-making art is not wanting. It can readily be shown that the earliest, as a class, even of arrow-heads, are ruder than the later, and the discovery of jasper had very much the effect, but in a less degree, that the discovery of iron had upon a bronze-age people. The occurrence of rude implements has been explained, or the attempt, at least, has been made to do so, by pronouncing every palæolithic implement as an unfinished neolithic weapon or tool; a purely gratuitous assumption. Where such rude implements are found in remarkable abundance, such places are designated as "workshops," where the material was tested, and if found available, carried to "finishing sites." We are taken to the former, and can follow in imagination the ancient miner digging into the hillside for suitable pebbles, but the "finishing sites" are so very vague as not to be available for archæological study; and in the best known of these localities, where only rude, palæolithic-like implements are found, not a trace as yet has been discovered of the Indian. This absence of pottery, arrow-points, and fragments of a pipe, are so far significant, that we have no valid reason to set forth, as has been done, that "rude implements" are unfinished objects and the refuse of late Indian industry. Admitted that they *may be* in some localities, still it has not been proven; and the evidence of the whole continent sets aside the rash inferences drawn from a single locality.

Admitting that to discriminate between an unfinished neolithic implement and a palæolithic one is always a difficult and sometimes an impossible feat, is not to acquiesce to the proposition that nothing truly palæolithic in character is found in America. If such objects are found in Europe, then it is true of America also ; for the distinction between American and European finds, such as is claimed by some, does not exist. To accept the view that palæolithic man once existed in other continents, and to refuse the evidence of his one-time presence here, is a violation of every canon of common sense. To claim that stone implements found imbedded in American gravel deposits, that are in every feature identical with those found in European gravels, are something other than palæolithic, and yet assent to the proposition of the existence of palæolithic man, is simple silliness and not science.

I have said that the most reasonable explanation must in all cases be accepted, and if the supposed palæolithic implements found in the river-bed and along the shore of Burlington Island be held as not of recent origin, what are the grounds for this view? Although these have been gone over many times, it is proper that the question be again discussed, as I am now treating of a region beyond the scope of earlier publications upon this subject. Then, too, there is opened up the subject of the archæological import of objects found on the exposed surfaces of gravel deposits ; and surface-found implements must always be more critically considered than those found at considerable depths in deposits. The latter, in spite of all the critics, scientific or otherwise, admit of no doubt as to their significance ; but does the river offer evidence of palæolithic man independent of these? The conditions under which these rude implements are found, point, first, to the fact that they were not made where they now occur. There are too few chips or spawls associated with them, and very seldom is a specimen collected that has not all the evidence of being a finished object. The base and cutting edge or point, or the two combined, are well defined. Where secondary chipping has been resorted to, to straighten and sharpen the edge, the defining boundaries of the delicate chips detached have been water-worn until nearly obliterated, and the condition of the entire surface has the same gloss that is a uniform feature of the associated pebbles.   It may be said that this result of water action is soon acquired; but, admitting this, the fact is still of value, in association with other conditions to be mentioned.   As an instance, similar implements from the gravel *in* the island, that have not been exposed to the water, except during the brief period of their transportation by a flood, are dull and lustreless.   Now it is difficult to conceive how the implements in the bed of the river and on the beach, covered and uncovered by the inflowing and outgoing tide, could have gotten to their present position, except by being associated with the gravel when it was deposited, or immediately afterwards, when Man had no other tool than this, and when the island was but a gravel bar.   In time, the action of the river has been to uncover and water-polish some, while those on the island and not so subjected are like the exposed argillite rock, of which they are made, where it is in place.   If these objects are of recent Indian origin, how did so many get into the river, where it now flows, and others find their way beneath the overlying sand and soil that forms the surface of the island?   If Indian implements of two or three centuries ago, or unfinished implements, it matters not, the evidence goes to show that what these people did not take pains to bury, they threw into the water — which is simply absurd.   There must necessarily have been localities in the upper Delaware valley where these objects were made, if no evidence can be found that they were made where now they occur, and this is wanting; and my conclusion is, that palæolithic implements found on the gravel of the island, in the bed of the river, and along the banks of the stream where the gravel is exposed, are a constituent part of that gravel, and were transported from certain up-river localities, in part; and others were left lying on the surface as it then was, or before the present overlying soils had begun to accumulate; and not until this present surface soil was nearly or quite what it is, did the use of pottery and specialized stone implements come into use.   This by no means calls for another than the Indian to mark the advent of man in the Delaware valley, but does

VIEW OF SECTION OF SAND DEPOSIT IN INTERIOR OF ISLAND.

call for, and every calmly considered fact demonstrates, that between the period when Man first appeared upon the scene and the day of his discovery by European adventurers, he slowly passed from the palæolithic to the neolithic stage of culture.

Such a problem as that of the relative ages of the two classes of objects found in the same locality is necessarily a difficult one, even when happy chance has favored us in many ways. One difficulty that would be almost insuperable in the Delaware valley we have not to contend with ; that is, the mineralogical identity of the two assumed classes of objects. Had the first chipper of stone used jasper or quartz as did the last, then no skill would suffice to distinguish between the palæolithic implement of the ice age and the unfinished implement of a later day. Perhaps this is too strongly put ; but between many of the latter and all the former no difference could be pointed out. But the conditions here are otherwise. The palæolithic implements are of one material, and that which characterizes the highest phase of neolithic art is another; and, though an army of apparent objections are marshalled by those who clamor for more facts, I cannot see how this one statement, a fact beyond the shadow of a doubt, can be overturned. Wander where you will, in the immediate valley or over the hills beyond, wherever argillite occurs, there you will find the peculiar, rude, but unmistakably finished objects, and of argillite. Now, if at the beginning of the occupancy of the river valley by Man, both jasper and argillite were used, as they subsequently were, how is it that on such an area as the gravel base of Burlington Island we find the objects exclusively of the one material ? If a rock-transporting flood should now occur, and tons of material be carried from the rock-ribbed valley above and spread over the present surface of the island, there would be found argillite, jasper, and quartz arrow-points, chips, and flakes, with innumerable potsherds, because these are now intimately associated on the surface of the valley ; but when the floods came that built up that island, there was but the one form existing ; it was brought down, and *the material is argillite.* Herein we have the long-desired clue by means of which we can trace the Man of the Delaware valley backward to the beginning of his era. This fact is the key unlocking many a mystery, and with it the student is armed with skill equal to unravelling the tangled skein of events from the close of the glacial epoch to the present time.

So far, my work has been within the tide-water regions of the river, and now how far are the above conclusions borne out by studies of the conditions in the upper or non-tidal portions of the river?

This begins at Trenton, New Jersey, and from that point the stream presents a wholly different aspect. Everywhere there are rocks in place, many huge boulders clog the channel, the water is generally shallow and moderately swift. The volume of water varies greatly, and the stream becomes almost insignificant during July and August. At such times the bed is easily explored, and is found for many miles to consist of a deposit of gravel and sand identical with that in the tidal portion. The striking difference is that it now is a gravel much more closely connected with the bed of the river, and has but little extension beyond those narrow limits.

It should here be stated that the rock of which palæolithic implements are made is in place, some twenty-five miles above Trenton, New Jersey, and in the river valley from that point southward, fragments of it and rude implements occur in almost endless quantity. In many, perhaps the large majority of instances, the rude and elaborate implements, "failures," chips, and broken pottery are so intimately associated that nothing appears clearer than that all objects of aboriginal workmanship date from practically the same date. The two areas, the upper and the tidal portions of the valley, flatly contradict each other, and the question arises, which tells the true story? I do not think that the demands of archæologists would be satisfied upon presentation of tables of comparative reasonableness, and unless the contradiction can be made to appear apparent rather than real, the problem of the original peopling of the valley of the Delaware remains unsolved.

But what does the study of the upper or non-tidal portion of the valley really show? Let us consider the conditions under which stone implements now occur with reference to the known past; for in this matter it is not warrantable to take anything for granted. Let the undetermined date of Man's arrival in the river valley, post-glacial, if you choose, — there is no evidence that man originated on the spot, and abundant reason for believing that he did not, — and admit, as all must, that the point of original contact is undiscovered and undiscoverable, although we can accept as probable such a point of entrance to the valley as the traces of Man seem most distinctly to indicate as such; it is safe to assert that the whole area was not invaded by a "wave of migration" as broad as the valley is long, nor was it reached at every few miles by roving bands of men at different but not widely separated dates. Of course, if Man reached America during the existence of glaciers in the river valley, he lived below their southern range, and occupied the valley as the ice receded; but all things considered, as we must derive Man from Europe, by way of a land communication across what is now the north Atlantic ocean, it is safe to say that he reached this continent in pre-glacial times, when race-differentiation had not taken place. To consider him as post-glacial and yet palæolithic in condition, opens up many difficulties that pre-glacial antiquity effectually sets aside. What, at this late day, are left us as indications of what transpired thousands of years ago? Is there anything decipherable, or must we say "lost is lost, and gone is gone forever"?

Let us suppose that the valley was essentially the same then as now, and Man reached it at a point as far north as the occurrence in place of both jasper and argillite. Such man, as we know positively, was in his stone age; and having both the minerals or rocks named, equally accessible, he may be supposed to have used both materials from the beginning of his occupancy.

Let me here add parenthetically that I have elsewhere shown that jasper was systematically mined, while the argillite is an outcropping rock admirably adapted to stone implement manufacture.

Is it inherently probable that when there was material to be had in limitless abundance, of uniform excellence, that another rock would be laboriously quarried and selection made from the detached masses, except that after long experience the mined material, jasper, proved superior, or was prized because of its beautiful colors? Can we imagine the first men who ever saw the Delaware River setting about prospecting for something still better than what was at hand and equal to all their demands? It is clearly certain that the jasper quarries were discovered in time — and a very long time — after the river valley was reached; but from the very beginning of the present epoch, if not during the whole duration of the quaternary period, no one could have entered the valley of the Delaware at this point and not seen the argillite. It is as conspicuous as the river itself and the hills that hem it in. Is there not in this fact alone evidence all important that the argillite-chipping interest antedates that of jasper working so decidedly that the difference in time is of archæological significance? I cannot think otherwise.

But be this as it may, as early Man wandered up and down the valley, he would scatter the products of his handiwork everywhere he went. Not a hearth but will have potsherds with the charcoal and ashes, and every village site will be marked by broken implements. These discarded tools or weapons, some of jasper, and others of argillite, will be found in practically equal numbers scattered everywhere that the people who used them reached. Whether on the seacoast or in the mountains, along the river or in the valleys of the inland creeks, it matters not; their spears, scrapers, knives, pottery, and pipes will everywhere be found. No one will be justified in saying of these objects, this was of yesterday, that of the day before. The Indian came, ages long ago, and remained until the white man drove him away: this is the whole story. But do we find the relics of aboriginal Man throughout the whole extent of the valley of the Delaware, as I have described? Is it, as made, a statement applicable to the whole valley and eastward to the sea? How, accepting it, can we explain the conditions that in preceding pages have been pointed out as really obtaining? If jasper and argillite implements were made on the same day, — that is, always, since implement-making began, — lost by the same individual or were carried by the same flood from the hills above, to the tide-water islands below, and to the long reaches of gravelly river beach, how does it happen that their dissociation occurs in so marked a manner as has been described; and how is it that the disputed palæolithic objects are more than ninety-nine per cent. of argillite, if the flint quarries at Durham and the argillite outcropping at Point Pleasant, a few miles away, were at the same time the busy scenes of implement-making? .

But it is urged that upon clearly defined village sites the common forms of chipped stone implements made, some of jasper, and others of argillite, are found so intimately associated that to assign to them different origins is absurd. This is unquestionably true, and I am not aware that it has ever been attempted. On the other hand, we must remember, as I have pointed out in the *Popular Science Monthly* for January, 1883, and again in December, 1889, that the argillite arrow-points — a distinctly neolithic, Indian implement — did *also* occur under two conditions that strongly suggested, if they did not prove, their use by Man prior to the general introduction of quartz and jasper. I showed, first, as a reason for this, "their occurrence in so many localities at a greater depth than that at which jasper and quartz arrow-heads are found. In other words, the plough unearths the Indian relics (*i.e.* relics of the later Indians) in great quantities; but, by digging deeper, objects of argillite are found in significant numbers;" and secondly, that localities could be traced where the use of argillite had been an exclusive one; village sites, or where a little cluster of wigwams once had stood, whose occupants had met every requirement of their simple lives without a trace of jasper, quartz, or silicious stone of any kind. Again, it has been pointed out that where implements were made from pebbles gathered from the bed of the river, there never occurred a trace of argillite, although, as boulders, that material is even more abundant than jasper, and I have never, in the tidal region of the Delaware valley, found an argillite workshop ; but, scattered promiscuously over very wide areas, often where no other trace of early man is found, are small flakes of argillite in great number, suggesting that when, ignorant of flint-like stone and probably not living in villages, a wanderer little above the beasts of the field, Man chipped this yielding stone to meet immediate wants, and discarded the rude object on accomplishing a present need. Unquestionably, argillite implements in Southern New Jersey, on the Pennsylvania shore of the Delaware River, and in Delaware and Northern Maryland, are far more widely distributed than are those of jasper and quartz. They occur wherever the latter do, and over all the intervening territory. If one will go over every foot of the ground that I have mentioned, and will pass thousands of cubic yards of shifting sands through a sieve, will give heed to all the circumstances surrounding the unearthing of every specimen, he will be thoroughly convinced that an argillite-using Man wandered far and wide over this country long before the use of jasper and quartz became so universal.

Can we reconcile this with the conditions that are found common to that region where the two minerals are found in place ? I do not think we have to seek far for the explanation. The main difficulty heretofore has been that the valley, as a whole, was not studied before venturing to express an opinion. The study of a single village site may sadly mislead us. Humanity is less fixed in habit than the lower animals, and an occurrence at one village, of which abundant evidence might remain — as a cannibal feast — might never have happened elsewhere ; yet how natural from one such exploration to conclude that cannibalism was a common, everyday matter. The explanation is, I maintain, that the discovery of jasper and allied mineral did not bring about the discarding of argillite, and that subsequently both materials were in use. Admitting this, the conditions in the tidal portion of the river valley are intelligible; otherwise they are not. This calls for evidence in the region where argillite is in place and was worked, of prolonged occupation of the locality by Man, and evidence, too, of the transition from simple to elaborate implement-making. Fortunately this is not wanting, or perhaps it would be more modest to state that what is believed to be such evidence is at hand.

Where the river, through the shifting of its current, has receded from one bank and washed bare some spot previously covered with soil and even supporting vigorous tree-growth, we often find, when the waters have returned to an older channel, that the denuded area is covered with an enormous quantity of minute chips, broken implements, fragments of pottery, and all that stamps a locality as a one-time village site. Here will be found flakes of argillite and splinters of jasper, and with them unfinished as well as broken chipped implements. This is important. Such unfinished objects at once catch the eye from their general resemblance to the palæolithic implements proper; but it does not follow that such resemblance proves them identical. As at Flint Ridge, Ohio, and at Durham, Pennsylvania, there are objects that might, if found elsewhere, puzzle the most expert; but they form an insignificant proportion of the great mass of discarded material with which they are associated. So little, indeed, that they are proven, by reason of their numbers, to be accidental merely. If a large series from a village site is taken and placed side by side with the forms they suggest, found in such a locality as the base of Burlington Island, or the great gravel deposit at Trenton, New Jersey, a difference not to be shown in a handful of specimens is apparent to every one familiar with stone implements of primitive types. The unfinished character of the one series is wanting in the other. The ultimate purpose, the fashioning of a recognized type of neolithic or later Indian implement is recognized. Taken as a whole, unfinished implements suggest no useful purpose, neither cutting edge or penetrating point being distinctly defined. On the other hand, a typical palæolithic implement has its value, even in our eyes. It is evidently better adapted to every conceivable use than any stone that, however fashioned by natural agencies, could be gathered from a gravel bank or the river bed ; and this cannot be said of unfinished implements, such as we find where flint chipping has been carried on. As has been remarked of European drift implements, they are "as clearly works of *art* as an Sheffield whittle," and as Lubbock reminds us, they "speak for themselves." But in the manufacture of any large implement, whether of earlier or later origin, failures must invariably and frequently occur, and how can we distinguish where no difference exists? We cannot, nor does the archæologist ever attempt it? When objects are removed from the ground to the museum cases, there is no possibility of determining their history. They lose that power to "speak for themselves" which is theirs, when, in the field, we gather them with a mind alert to every condition of their surrounding. Not even the camera can catch the significance that surrounds them. On such a village site every object must be compared with that with which it is associated. At such places, an unbroken series can be had from the most delicate arrow-point to the blocked-out mass of mineral. The chips, splinters, and spawls are all one with the finished product. The chips and splinters, particularly, are very small, as a rule. Ninety per cent. of them will measure less than an inch in any direction, and thousands of flakes are scattered through the soil not half that measurement and as thin as wrapping-paper. These are the resultant refuse scattered by workmen skilled in the production of highly specialized forms of tools and weapons, and not the flakes thrown off in shaping the most primitive form of implement of which we have any knowledge. It is much the same difference that we find between chips when a log is squared with an axe and the curled shavings of a modern planing mill.

The two materials, it must be borne in mind, jasper and argillite, are mingled, and probably in equal quantities. On the other hand, where argillite occurs alone, there is no such vast abundance of minute chips. Everything is on a larger or coarser scale, and, curiously enough, we find here certain types of rude implements, clearly a finished product, which are not reproduced in jasper. Again, all localities, where both minerals were worked, — and they are very numerous,— come well within the soil-making period. There is not a jot or tittle of evidence that their antiquity, great as it is in years, approaches the time of the glaciers' final disappearance.

But let us a little further into the channel of the river, or, following a land-slide, delve deeper into sloping hillsides, or, aided by excavations made by man, work what was once an inhabited and inhabitable surface ages long ago. What have we there? Taking advantage of the extremely low stage of water, careful search in the present bed of the river, — and this has been the bed for many centuries, — has revealed more than one locality where mingled with boulders, or rather, the latter partly covering and concealing them, were found not only typical palæolithic implements of argillite, but often the large flakes detached in their making, and not a trace of an "Indian" relic ; not a chip, large or small, of jasper. Nowhere have jasper implements been found under like circumstances ; never the many forms of an Indian's outfit. The boulders are here too large to have been moved by torrents of recent date, and the palæolithic implements about and even under them were not intrusive. The whole surroundings are eloquent of remote antiquity ; but while they weave a subtle spell that impresses the student when afield, add nothing of that cunning to his hand needful to record in fitting terms the story told by these minor monuments that Time hath spared. The same is true of such exposures of land surface as I have mentioned. If they reveal any trace at all of Man, it is of Man nearer to his primitive condition than the jasper-using Indian. Not that I would have inferred that the Indian, as he figures in the dawn of American history, has himself no history. That his tarrying in the land is a matter of many centuries is beyond a doubt. The studied effort to minimize the age of every object or event connected with him is as uncalled for as illogical, for upon general principles antiquity is admitted. It is, of course, a matter of "Time relative," and not "Time absolute"; but if we speak of the "Indian" in terms of years, then we must refer to his argillite-using ancestors in terms of centuries. Certainly, if as more and more generally asserted, the glacial period closed its disastrous activity some ten thousand years ago, then in the enormous area southward of its boundary Man must have existed and flourished for a very long time; as the evidences of Man upon this continent, his growth in many directions, his many languages and marked racial differentiation require a far longer lapse of years than that mentioned.

Great have been the changes in the upper valley of the Delaware since Man first appeared within it. Its narrow channel choked, the river has flooded many a plain until the new-made lake figures in the people's folk-lore, and then swiftly, as it came in being, the waters have disappeared, and the event is forgotten. With all these changes about him, the dusky hunter of the Delaware has not stood still. Changes have come to him to the bettering of his condition, until he looks backward with wonderment that his grandfathers could have been content with such primitive methods, such simple tools. Had the first bold European adventurer that entered this valley questioned the old men that he met, they would have told him, I believe, much the same story as I have here recorded, as drawn from scattered bits of broken stone; a story told here among the mountains quite the same as that the valley tells us when we near the sea. Another and most important phase of this subject calls, too, for reference, because of its archæological significance. A condition that I have believed would ultimately be demonstrated, has at last been shown to have existed in fact, and not theory. On the assumption that the river, when its valley was first occupied by Man, flowed at a higher level than at present, we should find in some localities where the ruder, argillite objects occurred at a higher level than the jasper implements made by the Indians at a date as recent as the shrinking of the stream until it only filled, except at freshet stages, its present bed. This is precisely what has been discovered both in the upper, non-tidal, and tidal portions of the river, and so explains how, by the crumbling of the banks of the stream, the two forms of relics have become commingled; the older, argillite objects being at a higher horizon, having fallen down among the more recent jasper handiwork of the later Indian, left by him at a lower level.

There are localities where a low bluff, some twelve to twenty feet high, extends parallel to the river's present course, and intervening a low meadow-like reach of sloping shore, but little above the ordinary level of the flood-tide. On this are found the ordinary traces of a one-time village site,—the spear and arrow-point, potsherds, grooved axes, the notched net-sinker, and scores of less well-defined forms of stone implements and weapons. These are all essentially "Indian" in origin, and may have been left, where now found, but three or four centuries ago. But on going back from the river and to the foot of the bluff I have mentioned, we find projecting from its face (of course only in some localities) the fairly well specialized argillite implements that I have persistently offered as the evidence of the intermediate period between the palæolithic era and that of the Indian as the European adventurer found him, a condition that may be described as post-palæolithic and pre-neolithic. This is unavoidably vague, perhaps, for the transition from lower to higher "culture" was so gradual that no hard and fast lines can be drawn; still it will aid, I hope, in making clear my general meaning. Of course the ordinary effects of exposure of any unprotected bluff is to loosen its materials and scatter them along its base, and necessarily in such an instance, as I have just described, these argillite or older objects, that were buried when the Indian dwelt upon the river-shore, are now to a greater or less extent mingled with them.

In the high, narrow, rocky valley of the non-tidal portion of the river,—and the same is true of the in-flowing creeks,—Man could and did, at first, only dwell in localities that were safe from the sudden rises of the wildly rushing stream. Here, far above the level of these creeks and the river, were left many objects of primitive Man's handiwork. They have but to be displaced by any agency to fall down to the near banks of the water of to-day, and what more likely than that they should fall upon sites where the Indians dwelt within even historic times? With rude pottery and jasper arrow-heads we find iron and brass tomahawks, and why not at such places find, too, the oldest traces of aboriginal Man, as well as the most recent. The arrow-head, as a rule, is older than the metal hatchet; why not the palæolithic implement older than the arrow-head?

A word more before dismissing the subject. I have purposely refrained from referring to the subject of palæolithic implements as found in place in undisturbed gravel deposits. Everything concerning the antiquity of Man on the Atlantic coast of North America, it is claimed by all, hinges upon such discoveries; but I do not believe it, and possibly will always stand alone in this. On the contrary, I submit the above results of the past summer's study of the valley of the Delaware as sufficient evidence, first, that Man was here as early as the formation of such islands as those I have named, and left upon their surfaces, prior to the accumulation of the soil, his only weapon, a palæolithic implement; and that during the soil-making period his skill increased and the more specialized forms of implements resulted; and not until the valley became practically what it now is, with its present fauna and flora, were the jasper mines discovered and the use of that material everywhere adopted. There is no evidence of a hiatus. Argillite, as material for implements, was never discarded. The presence in the great gravel deposits at the head of tide-water, and for miles beyond, of palæolithic implements, confirms this merely, I hold, but is not required to prove such sequence of condition and career of prehistoric man in the Delaware valley as I have here set forth.

Happily not all of the results of explorations in the valley of the Delaware call for discussion, and assuming that the preceding pages rightly set forth the very beginnings of human activity in the regions under consideration, will proceed to recount, in briefest manner, a few of the prominent results of a long summer's outing. These, it should be understood, are very largely the combined results of painstaking field work of Henry C. Mercer, Esq., of Doylestown, Pennsylvania, and of Mr. Charles Laubach, of Riegelsville, Pennsylvania, myself being much of the time a mere on-looker. To them, therefore, is due the credit of bringing to the attention of archæologists at large those facts concerning which a few remarks are in place, although a detailed report of the work accomplished is in course of preparation, but may be delayed, if another year in the field appears necessary.

Burial Customs

Inasmuch as our knowledge of the later Indians' customs are very largely to be gathered from the scattered relics found not only on but in the soil, it is evident that an all-important matter is to discover such localities as have not been disturbed since Indian times, and from them bring to light the remaining traces of their handiwork, so that we can learn to what extent certain objects were associated, and, possibly, through such association gain some insight as to the purpose of various patterns of implements, that of themselves do not indicate the uses to which they were put. Burial places, therefore, demand the closest inspection. In Smith's *History of New Jersey* (1765) we find it recorded that "it was customary with the Indians of West-Jersey, when they buried their dead, to put family utensils, bows and arrows, and sometimes money (wampum) into the grave with them, as tokens of their affection. When a person of note died far from the place of his own residence, they would carry his bones to be buried there ; they washed and perfumed the dead, painted the face, and followed singly ; left the dead in a sitting posture, and covered the grave pyramidically. They were very curious in preserving and repairing the graves of their dead, and pensively visited them." As the above was written at a time when information of this kind could be had at first hands, and was gathered by a very careful historian, it can be accepted as a simple statement of a fact, and the question now arises, how far is it borne out by the examination of localities which are known to have been long occupied by the Indians?

Probably nowhere east of the Alleghany Mountains and north of Virginia have traces of the aborigine proved more abundant than the face of the bluff forming the east bank of the Delaware River, between Trenton, New Jersey, and Bordentown, New Jersey, some five miles distant down the stream. From the fields immediately adjoining the writer's former home have been gathered, probably at this date, fully fifty thousand stone implements, and yet not any significant proportion of them have been derived from graves. As a rule, all these objects were exposed by the plough. Yet as there exists every indication of not only at one time a very large town having been here, but that it stood here for a protracted period, burials were necessarily very numerous, and the burial places not far distant. Indeed, the history of the locality as derived from the relics found here evidence clearly that the spot was a central one, and bones of those who died far from the place of their residence were doubtless continually brought here.

A recent very careful re-examination [1] of the entire region convinces me that a very considerable proportion of what are now surface-found relics are in reality grave-contents. That is, the objects were not left lying about by the Indians when discarded for others of European origin. To some extent this would be true; but as a rule, I believe, the stone axe, the shapely spear, the polished celt, and symmetrical gorget were placed, as Smith has mentioned, in graves and have since been

---

[1] My original report on the archæology of this portion of the valley of the Delaware is embodied in my work *Primitive Industry*, Salem, Mass., 1881, and in various articles in the *Popular Science Monthly*, D. Appleton & Co., New York, and in *Reports of the Peabody Museum of American Archæology*, Cambridge, Mass.

scattered by the general upturning of the surface of the land in the course of its cultivation by the European settlers. Occasionally a grave and its contents are brought to light, and while some of these confirm Smith's statement to the letter, there is found that other graves were made for a body only, for we cannot think they were robbed, and other localities show that several bodies were placed pell-mell in a single pit.

I have recently had brought to my notice the results of extensive excavations made along the river, when the Delaware and Raritan Canal was built, in 1832, and of the removal of a large natural mound in the meadows near by some years earlier. There were many skeletons exhumed, and associated with them in most instances many objects of native handiwork, and, curiously enough, quantities of copper. Now, if we were to judge of the use of copper by the Delaware Indians, by the number of objects made of this metal, found on the surface of ploughed fields, we would conclude that it was about the rarest of their possessions ; but the truth is the copper that was left behind by the Indians found its way to the melting-pot soon after the European came in possession of the land. Nor must we conclude that the occasional beautiful ceremonial.object, etched gorget, or carved bone ornament that we find at this late date, was always an object of rare occurrence even when the Indian was at the height of his prosperity. Such objects were common enough when the white settlers arrived, but, alas, there were no archæologists in those days, and such priceless treasures, as they would now be, were given as playthings to the children. I have positive knowledge of this being true, even so late as the beginning of the present century. To discover then by happy chance, the grave of an important personage among the early Indians, merely tells us, it may be, that his personal effects were many, elaborate, and perhaps artistic, but does not prove that he stood alone as an aboriginal Crœsus, or was a "mighty king" among his people. No grave has been recently opened, or is any likely to be discovered that will give us additional knowledge or prove that at any time, among the

Indians, there were individuals who were so pre-eminent while living as to be worthy of the name or title of "king."   Of petty chiefs there were scores.

Burial mounds, such as occur in Ohio, appear to be wanting in the tidal portion of the Delaware River valley, but such mounds are continually reported.   So far as my own examination of these so-called "mounds" extends they have proved in every case to be natural hillocks, which have been utilized as burial places.   Many of these hillocks have a curiously artificial appearance, but a study of the surrounding country shows how they have been formed by water carrying away here a little and there a little, until a conical mass of earth is left standing in a little plain.   That such a hillock should at once attract the Indian's attention is most natural.   That he should select its summit as the site of his home equally so, and where he long lived, there would an Indian be buried.   His direct descendants would surely, if it were practical, be interred in this hill whereon their parent or remote ancestor had dwelt.   One such hillock, recently removed, contained faint traces of very ancient burials, and it appeared as if a dozen or fifteen individuals at least had here been laid to rest by their people.

EARTHWORKS

It has been held of late years, and with apparently good reason, that the Indians of the Delaware valley,—the Lenni Lenâpé,—whatever the particular subdivision of the nation, were not "Mound Builders."   Nothing akin to a mound, square, circle, or simple embankment has been put on record in archæological or historical literature, and yet when we consider the needs of a people living in a state of almost perpetual warfare, —their foes, the Iroquois, were not so very far away,—it becomes evident that some other method than mere alertness must have been adopted to avoid surprise, and the simple method of protective earthworks was doubtless in use at various points up and down the river. There was, it has been stated,[1] such an enclosed area—a long, narrow strip of several acres surrounded by an earth embankment—on the brow of the bluff forming the east bank of the river, immediately south of Trenton, New Jersey. Not a trace of this now remains. Small, conical hillocks, possibly artificial, but probably not, were used as burial places, and have been occasionally referred to as mounds, but such as I have examined in Southern New Jersey did not present conclusive evidence of an artificial origin.

It was not altogether a matter of surprise to me, therefore, when I had reported to me, by Messrs. Mercer and Laubach, that they had found abundant evidence that the Delaware Indians were builders of mounds. Mr. Laubach found that near most of the village sites in the upper valley of the Delaware that he examined there were conical earth-mounds or "observatories," as he designates them. He writes: "In one instance, three circular mounds of about thirty feet in diameter and six feet in height occur near a supposed burning-place, where possibly human remains were cremated, and near also a well-defined Indian field. These mounds, when dug away, proved to contain nothing. That they were artificial was evident, but nothing in or about them suggested for what purpose they were used by the Indians."

Mr. Mercer found during the summer abundant evidence that the Lenni Lenâpé were "to a considerable extent, builders of mounds." He has reported a series of eight artificial mounds in a low meadow near Wieder's Creek, between three and four hundred yards north of the jasper quarry. One of these on examination proved to contain burnt stones and large quantities of charcoal. A series of irregularly located mounds in close proximity to certain stone "fire-pits" and a paved area, near

---

[1] "A little below the falls of Delaware on the Jersey side, at Point-no-Point in Pennsylvania, and several other places, were banks that have been formerly thrown up for intrenchments against incursions of the neighboring Indians, who, in their canoes, used sometimes to go in warlike bodies from one province to another."— HOWE AND BARBER, *Hist. Coll. of New Jersey.*

Bridge Point. Four mounds, the remaining ones of probably one hundred reported to have been destroyed by cultivation. These are on the right bank of a creek in Lehigh County, Pennsylvania. Mr. Mercer also found mounds on Hexenkopf Mountain, and a series of thirteen near the jasper quarry on Rattlesnake Hill.

What part these earthworks played in the Lenâpéan economy can only, as yet, be conjectured. Their purpose, as in mounds in Ohio, is not expressed by their contents, not one that has been examined having shown any connection with mortuary customs. On the contrary, they were apparently made use of after they were built, and so the term "observation mound" used by Mr. Laubach is a warranted one.

Stone Mounds — Paved Areas — Standing Stones

Circular heaps of stones, paved areas, and upright slabs of stone are very substantial facts in the experience of the field archæologist, in that portion of the Delaware valley immediately south of the junction of the Delaware and Lehigh rivers. Probably their occurrence is over a much more extensive tract. That they are in every instance the work of Indians is evident ; but how far are we justified in accepting the unvarying local tradition, that refers them to mortuary customs? Mr. Mercer has reported to me " several stone-paved fire-sites arranged in groups and covering areas more than one hundred paces square." He states : "Mr. Laubach and myself found a tumulus made of small stones, with a large rectangular block of stone protruding vertically from near the middle, about eighteen inches above the surrounding small stones ; and near by, in a dense growth of timber, a score of artificial depressions partly sur-rounded with heaps of the excavated earth. The depressions were lined with loose stones, and contained charcoal, finely powdered, lumps of brownish, waxy mold, and fire-cracked and scorched stones."

At two other localities, areas one hundred yards in diameter were paved with stones placed lengthwise on edge. Here, also, charcoal, ashes, and other evidences of fire were seen.

Mr. Mercer suggests, after a careful examination of many of these places, that they were not connected with ordinary every-day life, because of

"The absence about the fire-pits of fractured animal bones, pottery, and the various forms of stone implements common at village or temporary camp sites.

"The large spaces covered by the artificial stone flooring, and the situation of these places upon hill-tops, at inconvenient distances from water, and where the exposure to the wind made wigwam life impracticable.

"The frequent occurrence of charcoal and ashes, one or both."

These are all reasons worthy of consideration, and certainly the bare evidence of fire in ashes and charcoal has a deep significance, in that such fire was doubtless a ceremonial one. As Mr. Mercer suggests, the evidence of every-day life being absent, we must look for an explanation of these paved areas in the extraordinary affairs of the Indian, and what, indeed, more probable, than their association exclusively with burial rites? "Their greatest festival was held in honor of Fire, which they personified," writes Dr. Brinton, and we can readily believe this, even were there no documentary evidence to such effect, when we come to examine the localities where these people dwelt for many centuries. Did not many circumstances lead to the conviction that these circles of stones, paved areas, and stone mounds point to their intimate association with mortuary customs, they would still be of exceeding interest. Mr. Laubach, who called attention to these stone heaps, writes me that "it is well known in the neighborhood [*i.e.* tradition from father to son] that fires were lit after dark, and dancing about them, with fearful howls and yells, was continued all night." "The Indians met," he says, "on certain hill-tops at stated intervals, and about huge bon-fires, celebrated certain rites, which the early European settlers were given to understand had reference to their dead." It is evident, I think, that whatever method was adopted in disposing of their dead, these stone-paved areas, stone mounds, and standing stones, bore intimate relation to their mortuary customs.

JASPER QUARRIES

Early in the summer of 1891 Mr. Laubach, to whom American archæologists are much indebted, conducted Mr. H. C. Mercer, of the University's Archæological Museum, and myself to the source, or one of them, from which the Delaware Indians derived their jasper, of which the finer and later chipped stone implements were made. The quarries are situated about one mile east of the village of Durham, Bucks County, Pennsylvania, in the synclinal basin of Rattlesnake and Mine Hill, on the lowermost spur of the South Mountain range. They cover an area of about one acre. Some forty or more years ago these quarries were exposed or open, so that the mineral could be plainly seen, but of late every excavation has become the receptacle for refuse stone gathered from the adjacent fields. When first seen by Mr. Laubach, the exposures of the jasper were from four to six feet in depth, and from ten to twenty feet in diameter. In close proximity, in every case, the *débris* was heaped about the openings so as to form a prominent, mound-like elevation. The greater or less depth to which the excavations were carried on was doubtless owing to the superior or inferior quality of the exposed ledges.

Immediately east of the quarries was, in earlier years, a never-failing spring forming a small, circular pond. Now it has disappeared, having been tapped by the mining operations of the Durham Iron Company. This spring no doubt furnished water both for domestic and mining purposes, as there is abundant evidence that the locality was permanently occupied, and water and fire were the means used, it is inferred, to detach and break up the mineral, so that it could be conveniently transported to the several implement-making sites in the immediate neighborhood.

Subsequently, Mr. Mercer visited the locality and made most thorough examination of this locality. As a result of his explorations, he has concluded : —

1. The jasper does not occur at any of the quarries in solid veins,[1] but at each lies imbedded in clay in natural nodules, varying in size from three inches to five feet in diameter.

2. The finest jasper lies at or near the surface; none of the prehistoric excavations probably having had a greater depth than four or five feet at most.

3. The Indians could generally find nodules near enough the desired size to save themselves the trouble of reducing large blocks.

4. Some of the pits were used as fire-sites for cooking, in which, with charcoal and scorched stones, I found the bones of mammals. Also, the numerous large masses of burnt jasper at the quarry proves fire to have been common about the edges of pits.

5. The smaller pit at Durham, consisting of a bottom layer of nodules of inferior quality and much altered by heat, and interspersed with charcoal and chips of the finest jasper, may have been used as an oven for splintering large lumps of the best quality laid on the top. Now, only the chips remain.

6. The reddened lumps — the jasper is naturally of various shades of yellow and brown — seem to denote that, in some cases, the Indians may have purposely changed the color into red by fire, though in my experience the process seemed to injure the quality of the mineral.

It will be noticed that the views of Mr. Laubach and of Mr. Mercer are somewhat at variance, but not materially so, and both agree in the view, as stated at the outset, that we have

---

[1] Mr. Laubach writes: "The jasper is found at present in the position and condition specified by Mr. Mercer. When, however, discovered by primitive man, it was no doubt exposed in a solid, ledge-like dyke. Following this outcrop of jasper nodules to a greater depth, they will be found harder and resembling the appearance of jaspery hematite iron ore, and beyond this the rock would assume a real ledge-like aspect, as can be seen at the new surface tunnel, where the jasper vein is nearly fifty feet in thickness."

here, on the bank of the river, one of the sources from which jasper was procured by the Indians. It is not the only one discovered, however, during the past summer. Mr. Mercer found and carefully explored another some miles off, in Lehigh County, Pennsylvania. It, too, is on a hill, at an altitude of five hundred feet above tide.

The objects obtained therefrom consist of a large number of chips of artificial origin and of fractured nodules, colored **far** more variously than the specimens of like character from the Durham quarries. They are light and dark yellow, brown, olive-green, red, rose, pink, white, black, and veined in various tints, and account for nearly, if not all, the variety of color occurring in jasper implements as discovered in the Delaware valley and regions thereabouts for many miles.

Village Sites

Throughout the preceding pages will be noticed many references to Indian village sites. Such spots are readily recognized by the character of the objects found thereon. Everything entering into the daily lives of its occupants occur, and, more noticeably than all else, innumerable potsherds. These one-time villages were named as our modern towns, the name usually being suggested by some peculiarity of locality. One of these, carefully explored by Mr. Laubach, was situated on the Delaware River, where Riegelsville, Bucks County, Pennsylvania, now stands. Its name was PECHOT-WOALHENK, signifying *where there is a great depression in the land.* This ancient village is of peculiar interest in that it was allotted to the Shawnees by the Delawares, and occupied by them from about 1690 to 1728.

Mr. Laubach has in past years gathered from this spot an enormous number of stone implements, weapons, ornaments, and indeed every form of Indian object. The collection, now in the Museum of the University of Pennsylvania, contains, besides finished objects, abundance of that refuse material indicating that the manufacture of arrow-points was extensively carried on,

Within the limits of this village was the remarkable cave of which portions still remain, and doubtless from this cave was derived the name of the village: Pechot-woalhenk, *where there is a great depression in the land.* It is located a little north of Durham Creek, and prior to 1848 "had a total length of about three hundred feet, an average height of twelve, and a breadth varying from ten to forty feet. The cave in its natural state was divided into three compartments or levels, each reached by descending a short incline of about ten feet. Some distance from the steep incline of the second level occurred a narrow lateral cavern terminating in the form of a letter T. One narrow passage led to a dark and gloomy room about eight feet by twelve in dimension. This is associated, locally, with the well-known " Indian Queen " or " Queen Esther," a half-breed Seneca woman, who, it is said, had great influence with the Indians of this region during her time.

That the cave was constantly occupied by Indians admits of no doubt, as very many implements, ornaments, and bits of pottery of aboriginal origin have been found in it.

Caves and rock-shelters were constantly utilized as dwelling-places in the valley of the Delaware, and their careful exploration is greatly to be desired. In the romantic valley of the Tohickon Creek Mr. Mercer and myself examined a simple shelter formed by the out-jutting of a ledge of rock, where evidences of frequent occupation were very abundant. Throughout the *débris* that covered the floor were the broken and charred bones of deer and wild turkey, fish, turtles, and also shells of the fresh-water mussels. Mingled with these were stone implements and abundant potsherds. I am indebted to the careful historic work of William J. Buck, Esq., of Jenkintown, Pennsylvania, for information with reference to this interesting rock-shelter.

Before concluding my reference to caves and rock-shelters, such as occur in the limestone and slate regions of the upper Delaware valley, I wish to call attention to another phase of cave-life among the Indians which has been overlooked. I refer to caves in the earth. If history does not mislead us, the early English settlers of Philadelphia and more than one family in New Jersey, in lieu of other shelter, took refuge in a cave. Even such places became permanent abodes, and it is recorded of one family that they dwelt in one on the bank of a creek "until nine children were born," when it is supposed this subterranean home became over-crowded. The question arises, Did the English take to caves of their own notion, or get the hint from the Indians? I have failed to find any reference to earth-homes among our Delaware Indians, and yet I have some reason to believe that such shelters were used. It has happened on more than one occasion that in the course of extensive diggings masses of charcoal and such traces of the Indian, as are found on the surfaces of fields, occur in considerable abundance in a very limited spot, and at a significant depth. Such "finds" have been explained away as the result of land-slides and other mildly cataclysmic occurrences, all of which are extremely improbable, or have been held up as evidence that we could get from relics no clue whatever to the question of the antiquity of the Indian. Where these deep-down "finds" occur on the side of a slope, or the face of a bluff, it is, I think, far more probable that there was once an artificial cave there, that, being abandoned, had gradually filled up. And in cases where these "finds" occur on what is now level ground, I can only suggest that for warmth, in winter, and to render them less conspicuous, the Indian dug circular pits of a few feet — four to six — and roofed them over, instead of a "wattled hut" or skin-covered wigwam. This would explain the few instances where large numbers of traces of the Indian have been found in the gravel and on the same horizon, in some cases, with the scanty traces of his distant ancestor, palæolithic Man.